Matthew Russell

Madonna

Verses on Our Lady and the Saints

Matthew Russell

Madonna

Verses on Our Lady and the Saints

ISBN/EAN: 9783337331191

Printed in Europe, USA, Canada, Australia, Japan

Cover: Foto ©Thomas Meinert / pixelio.de

More available books at **www.hansebooks.com**

MADONNA:

Verses on Our Lady and the Saints.

BY THE

REV. MATTHEW RUSSELL, S.J.

AUTHOR OF "EMMANUEL: A BOOK OF EUCHARISTIC VERSES."

"Sancta Maria et omnes Sancti intercedant pro nobis ad Dominum."
DIV. OFFIC. AD PRIMAM.

DUBLIN:
M. H. GILL & SON, 50 UPPER SACKVILLE-ST.
1880.

TO THE MEMORY

OF

A GOOD AND WISE MOTHER

WHO, WHEN ON EARTH, TAUGHT ME TO LOVE

Our Mother

WHO IS IN HEAVEN.

~~~~~~~~~~

"Do Thou, O Lord my God, inspire thy servants, my brethren, that so many as read these pages may, at thy altar, remember Monica, thy handmaid, with Patricius her husband, through whom Thou broughtest me into this life."—*St. Augustine's Confessions.*

Quand je pouvais encor vous voir et vous entendre,
   Quand, parmi vos travaux, ma mere, et vos douleurs,
Mon cœur de fils pouvait à vos pieds se répandre
   Et faire éclore en vous de la joie ou des pleurs ;

Avant l'heure où, brisant le bonheur domestique,
   Dieu vous plaça plus haut que nos amours humains,
Lorsque ma lèvre encor s'appuyait sur vos mains,
   Lorsque vous étiez là sur ce fauteuil antique :

Trop souvent de mon cœur j'ai retenu la voix ;
   Je vous ai trop peu dit, c'est là ma peine amère,
Ces choses qu'un bon fils doit dire mille fois
   Pour payer, s'il se peut, les peines d'une mère.
                                            Victor de Laprade.

While I could still behold thee, still could hear—
   While 'mid thy toils, my mother, and thy grief,
My filial heart might still have nestled near,
   And made thee seek in smiles or tears relief ;

Before that hour when, breaking our home-bliss,
   God placed thee high o'er human love and care—
While yet my lips thy gentle hand could kiss,
   While thou wast yonder in that quaint old chair :

Too often have I checked my heart's fond play,
   Too seldom said (keen now the pang I prove!)
What each true son a thousand times should say
   To pay (what can ?) the pains of mother's love.
                                            M. R.

PREFACE.

This little volume is intended as a companion to my book of Eucharistic Verses, "EMMANUEL," which was published two years ago, and which, after passing through four editions at home and in the United States, is now kept permanently in two forms—a sixpenny edition for more general use, and also the original neater edition reduced in price.

In the pages devoted to the saints, many names are absent which might naturally be sought for there. The reason is that almost all these verses found themselves written accidentally, for the most part many years ago, without any view to their forming items in a collection of this sort. I am not without hopes of being able to supply in a third series of "Altar Flowers" some of the omissions and shortcomings of this volume and its predecessor.

The first of the Anathematismi of St. Cyril, which were approved by the Council of Ephesus, may serve as a link between "EMMANUEL" and "MADONNA." *"Si quis non confitetur Deum veré esse Emmanuelem et propterea Dei genitricem esse sanctam virginem—peperit enim secundum carnem Verbum carnem factum—anathema sit."*—" If any one does not confess that God is truly Emmanuel [*God with us*] and that the Holy Virgin is therefore Mother of God—for she brought forth according to the flesh the Word made flesh—let him be anathema."

I earnestly commend "MADONNA" to the care of Her after whom I have dared to name it, as well as to the kind favour of the numberless sodalities of her children—*Enfants de Marie*—those especially in whose pious exercises it is my privilege to take part.

May, 1880.

CONTENTS.

	PAGE
Dedication	3
Preface	5
In Memoriam C. W. R.	9
Inscription	12
Our Lady's Magnificat	13
Memorare	18
A May Song	20
"Enfant de Marie"	21
To the Queen of May	23
The Madonna of the Schoolroom	25
Our Lady's Lamp	28
Rosary Rhymes	30
The Story of Mater Admirabilis	35
Our Lady's Office at Matins	43
To the Sacred Heart of Jesus	44
Dante's Prayer to the Blessed Virgin	45
Hymn to Mary Immaculate	47
The Name of Mary	50
Mother Most Pure	51
St. Joseph, our Father	53
Sonnet to St. Joseph	54
The Joys and Sorrows of St. Joseph	55
St. John the Baptist	58
St. Matthew	60
St. Mary Magdalen	64

CONTENTS.

	PAGE
St. Agnes	65
St. Emerentiana	67
St. Dorothy	69
St. Monica	73
St. Patrick	75
Blessed Imelda	79
St. Thomas Aquinas	82
St. Francis of Assisi	84
St. Francis de Sales	87
St. Ignatius Loyola	90
St. Aloysius Gonzaga	94
St. Stanislaus Kostka	96
Blessed John Berchmans	99
My Three	101
St. John Francis Regis	102
My Saints in Heaven	105
To My Angel	109
Aspirations	111
Colophon	112

APPENDIX.

Rhythmus ad SS. Cor Jesu	113
Ad B. V. Mariam sine labe conceptam	114
Il Nome di Maria Santissima	116
Irish Translation of the Poem at page 23	117

IN MEMORIAM

C. W. R.*

Our tongues are loosed, for thou art dead!
    Our hearts may utter what they feel.
We dared not, till thy spirit fled,
    Our worship and our love reveal.

But God has ended thy long pain,
    Thy term of forced repose is run.
Kind friends to keep thee strove in vain—
    God's will be done, God's will be done!

His gracious will had struck thee down
    While fruitfullest thy labours seemed:
For God would finish *thus* thy crown,
    And not as proud affection dreamed.

We dreamed thy ripened wisdom still
    Might train the *soggarths* of our race;
And that thy reverend form might fill
    For many a year its lofty place;

---

* "Pray for the soul of Charles William Russell, D.D., President of Maynooth College (1857-1880), who died, February 26th, 1880, in the 68th year of his age, and the 45th year of his priesthood."—*Mortuary Card.*

That thou wouldst spend thyself still more
   In serving all, thy aid who sought,
And using well the treasured lore
   By many a studious vigil bought.

But suddenly thy course is checked,
   Thy hand its toils reluctant stays;
And many a hope and plan are wrecked,
   'Mid sleepless nights and workless days.

Three patient years of painful rest
   Ere yet the generous heart grew still.
We wanted thee—but God knows best,
   And welcome be his holy will!

He would thy meek endurance prove,
   And so He willed thee long to be
The grateful object of that love
   Two kindred hearts poured out on thee:

Two faithful wedded hearts as pure,
   As rich, as noble as thy own—
(He will remember you, be sure,
   Dear friends, before the great white Throne).

Farewell! Thy strong and tender heart,
   Thy earnest will, thy spacious mind,
Had well and fully played their part,
   Though more, we thought, remained behind.

Much do we know, yet little know
  Of all the worth that filled thy days;
For thy fine nature hated show,
  Did good by stealth, and shrank from praise.

In spheres of duty wide apart,
  Thy calm, unresting zeal found scope;
Of many a home and many a heart
  The comfort thou and stay and hope.

Yet none of those who prized thee best
  To pain thee with their praise might dare;
And hearts with gratitude oppressed
  Could only whisper it in prayer.

But thou art gone! And *now* we may,
  Unchidden, all our love proclaim,
And vow, whilst we behind thee stay,
  To honour and to bless thy name.

Farewell! Whate'er the future brings
  To us—no longer by thy side—
'Twill urge us on to higher things
  To think that thou hast lived and died.

'Tis many a year since a little child
   Was wont to pore o'er the pages
That told the tale of virgins mild,
   Of martyrs and sainted sages,
Till he learned to love the saints above
   Like sisters and like brothers:
May his little book light up that love
   In his heart grown old, and others!

MADONNA.

OUR LADY'S MAGNIFICAT.

JESUS tacebat. Not alone
When at the last He would atone
By silence for our sinful speech—
Like lesson He was wont to teach
Throughout his toilsome exile here.

And She, most near to Him, most dear,
Learned well that lesson. Few the words
Which, sweet as innocent song of birds,
Fell from our Lady's lips; and they
Back into silence sank away,
Unnoted, save a phrase or two
Which Holy Writ keeps ever new.

Once only did her soul flow o'er:
When at her cousin's cottage door
Her grand *Magnificat* out burst.
And mark how calmly from the first

Her high exulting spirit soared:
"My soul doth magnify the Lord,
Who from on high hath deigned to bless
His lowly handmaid's lowliness.
Lo! henceforth generations all
Shall blessed and thrice blessed call
Me unto whom the Mighty One
Hath in his might such great things done."

Oh! God be praised who laid our lot
Within that Church which grudges not
The title thou thyself didst claim.
Yes, " Blessed Virgin" is the name
Which Christian hearts with joy bestow,
Thy prophecy fulfilling so.

We were before thy prophet-soul
When God the future did outroll
Distinct and clear before thine eye
In that meek hour of ecstasy.
Of *us* thou thoughtest, not of those
Who blame each word of praise that flows
From loving hearts in prayer to thee—
Who coldly carp and chide, while we
As God's true Mother bless thy name
And thee for our own Mother claim.

If scandals, heresies, *must* come,
'Tis well that sign there should be some

For all, and not a learned few,
To mark the false creed from the true,
Plain to all simple hearts and pure.
Thou, Mary, art that sign secure!
Scarce other "Note" faith's instinct needs
Than the Hail Mary and the Beads.
How, then, dares heresy to raise
A standard which itself betrays—
This jealousy of Her who bore
The Lord whom we and they adore?

Yes, all who love the Crucified
Must cherish her who stands beside,
To us in that dread moment given
As Mother, and who now in heaven,
Mother of Jesus glorified,
Within his heart and at his side
For ever holds a mother's place.
Hail, Queen of Heaven! Hail, full of grace!

Nor let the impious slanderer say
That Mary's clients turn away
The worship due to God alone,
And lift a creature to his throne.
Was e'er the vilest fanatic
Duped by this hideous, lying trick?
The simplest crone that tells her beads—
Her cross the only book she reads—

Knows well that She, upon whose breast
The Babe divine doth sweetly rest,
Is still a woman, meek and mild,
Though Jesus, Jesus, is her Child!

They, too, who raise this parrot-cry
Of a besotted bigotry,
Know well, themselves—for o'er and o'er
We've stooped to tell them—we adore
One only God, of lords the Lord,
Eternal Trinity, whose word
Made all created things to be,
And, foremost of mere creatures, Thee;
Thee, Mary, whom God raised so high
That saint and angel come not nigh.

Nay, they who Mary's prayers disdain,
If they the Christian name retain—
(Those wretched souls who half deny
Themselves, their Maker, we pass by)—
Believe or to believe pretend
That God once deigned on earth to send
His Son, co-equal God, to be
Our bloody ransom on the Tree;
And they believe that God as man,
Living and dying, wrought this plan—
True Man, true God, both then and now,
And his true Mother, Mary, thou!

Ye, then, who love the Child, for shame!
Blaspheme no more the sacred name
Of Mother, nor presume to part
Whom God for ever, heart to heart,
Hath joined as Son and Mother.
        Thou,
O Mother of my God, wilt now,
And always to my dying day,
Be unto me a Mother. Pray
That never till the day I die
May I by word or deed deny
The love which fills my heart and mind
For thee, true Mother of mankind!
And when thy Son the sign has given,
Take me, O Mother, home to heaven.

MEMORARE.*

REMEMBER, holy Mary,
  'Twas never heard or known
That any one who sought thee
  And made to thee his moan—
That anyone who hastened
  For shelter to thy care
Was ever yet abandoned
  And left to his despair.
No, never, Blessed Virgin,
  Most merciful, most kind!
No sinner cries for pity
  Who does not pity find.
    None, none, O holy Mary!

---

* Lest any reader should not have off by heart the prayer which has long been for so many hearts a prayer of predilection, we give it here :—

Memorare, O piissima Virgo Maria, non esse auditum a sæculo, quenquam ad tua currentem præsidia, tua implorantem auxilia, tua petentem suffragia, esse derelictum. Ego, tali animatus confidentia, ad te, Virgo virginum, Mater, curro. Ad te venio; coram te gemens peccator assisto. Noli, Mater Verbi, verba mea despicere, sed audi propitia et exaudi.

The following is one of the best of the English versions in use :—

Remember, O most gracious Virgin Mary, that never was it heard of in any age, that anyone who fled to thy protection, implored thy help, and sought thy intercession, was left unaided. Inspired with this confidence, I fly unto thee, O Virgin of virgins, my Mother. To thee I come; before thee I stand sinful and sorrowful. O Mother of the Word Incarnate, despise not my petitions, but in thy mercy hear and answer me.

And so to thee, my Mother,
  With filial faith I call,
For Jesus dying gave thee
  As Mother to us all.
To thee, O Queen of virgins!
  O Mother meek, to thee
I run with trustful fondness,
  Like child to mother's knee.
See at thy feet a sinner,
  Groaning and weeping sore—
Ah! throw thy mantle o'er me,
  And let me stray no more.
        No more, O holy Mary!

Thy Son has died to save me,
  And from his throne on high
His Heart this moment yearneth
  For even such as I.
All, all his love remember,
  And, oh! remember, too,
How prompt I am to purpose,
  How slow and frail to do.
Yet scorn not my petitions,
  But patiently give ear,
And help me, O my Mother,
  Most loving and most dear!
        Help, help, O holy Mary.

A MAY SONG.

'Tis May, 'tis May, the Month of Mary,
   The month that we have sighed for long;
And earth, so mute before, and dreary,
   Is bursting out in smiles and song.
The hedge-rows thrill with anthems gay,
And white lambs o'er the green fields play;
And earth and heaven keep holiday,
To welcome in the welcome May.

The gardens chant their odorous psalter
   To her, the mystic Queen of Flowers,
And lay with pride on Mary's altar
   The first-born of the sunny showers:
While censers breathe and organs play,
And sin and sadness pass away,
And skies are bright, and hearts are gay,
For this is Mary's own sweet May.

This dewy moon of buds we give her,
   From whom the Root of Jesse sprung—
Pure as the lily by the river,
   Joy o'er the mourning world she flung.
For as the day-star heralds day,
Her rising chased the clouds away,

And winter dared no longer stay
When Mary dawned—the Christian May.

A brighter Maytime blooms above us,
   With fairer flowers and richer sheen,
Where she with mother's love will love us,
   Who, there, as here, is crownèd Queen.
Ah! listen, Mary, while we pray—
Ah! take us to thy home one day;
Its summer ne'er shall fade away—
In heaven it shall be always May.

"ENFANT DE MARIE."

"CHILD OF MARY." Name of honour,
   Prouder far than kingly crown—
God Himself to win that title
   From his heavenly throne came down.
He the First-born Child of Mary
   Calls us to his Mother's side,
Shares with us his dearest treasure:
   "Mother, 'twas for these I died."

O Immaculate, unfallen,
   Tarnished by no breath of sin!
Yet I dare to call thee "Mother—"
   Open, Mother, let me in!

Thou of Mercy's self art Mother,
   And thy heart is meek and mild;
Open wide thy arms and take me
   As a mother takes her child.

God forgive those erring Christians
   Who would spurn the tender name
Which with joy, at Christ's own bidding,
   Mary's loving children claim.
"Lo, your Mother!" said He, dying;
   Yet some coldly turn away.
Ah! forgive them, sweetest Mother!
   For they know not what they say.

"Child of Mary." May my feelings,
   Thoughts, words, deeds, and heart's desires,
All befit a lowly creature
   Who to such high name aspires.
Ne'er shall sin (for sin could only)
   From my sinless Mother sever—
Mary's child till death shall call me,
   Child of Mary *then* forever.

TO THE QUEEN OF MAY.

O MARY, dearest Mother!
   Thy month is come again,
Of all the months most welcome
   To angels and to men—
The month of birds and blossoms,
   The flowery, sunny May,
When earth and sky, dear Mother!
   To thee fond tribute pay.

And so, O dearest Mother!
   Before the simple shrine
Which we have decked with flowers
   Because we call it thine,
We kneel to scatter incense
   And prayer and song for thee:
Look down, O dearest Mother!
   Look down to hear and see.

Look down on us thy children,
   O Mother dear! look down;
The mother's face beams kindly
   When other faces frown.
Though thou art Queen of Heaven,
   And reign'st in joy above,
Yet still, O dearest Mother!
   Look down on us with love.

Ah! we have forced thee often,
    All loving as thou art,
To turn in sadness from us,
    Thine eyes—but not thy heart!
In grief but not in anger,
    Though we have tried thee sore:
Yet smile again, dear Mother!
    We'll vex thy heart no more.

By Him who calls thee Mother,
    And bids us do the same—
By Him, thy Son, who gives us
    A brother's tender name—
By all the love that yearneth
    Within thine own pure heart,
O Mother! be a mother,
    And act a mother's part.

In Heaven's eternal May-time
    Whose sunlight is the Lamb,
In the gladness and the glory,
    The rapture and the calm—
We'll praise thee, and we'll bless thee,
    With happy saints above,
If now, O mighty Mother,
    Thou look on us with love.

THE MADONNA OF THE SCHOOLROOM.

Look! What is this sweet picture
    That beameth from the wall?
A Mother smiling kindly,
    Yet gravely, down on all;
A halo round her forehead—
    Through her heart a sword is drawn:
Ah! glow, my heart, with welcome—
    'Tis Mary looking on!

Has Mary come to frown us
    Into sober, sullen mood?
Ah! no. Although 'twould grieve her
    To see us wild or rude,
She loves us to be merry
    As kids on sunny lawn,
And feel like happy children
    Whose mother's looking on.

She knows God's hopes and wishes,
    She knows our daily task,
And watching how we do it,
    Her mild eye seems to ask:

"Ah! know ye not, my children,
  How soon your lives are gone?
Thus serve ye Him whose Mother
  From heaven looketh on?"

Have I so prayed and studied
  This week, this month, this year,
As pleased that watchful Mother
  And my angel standing near?
Well, God will deal in mercy
  With what is past and gone,
If now we strive in earnest,
  Since *she* is looking on.

If giddy comrades ever
  Should lure my mind away
From that which all who love me
  Desire from me to-day;
I'll firmly bid the tempter,
  How gay soe'er, begone—
"Ah! hush," I'll say; "be quiet,
  Our Mother's looking on."

Or worse—if slimy serpents
  Of earth or hell crawl near
To hiss their filth unholy
  Into my heedless ear—

I'll shrink from e'en their shadow,
   Fleet as the startled fawn:
"Foul fiend! I hate and scorn thee,
   For Mary's looking on."

But not in this scene only
   Of schoolboy work and play,
Nor in the homelike chapel
   Where we the Rosary say;
Not now alone but always,
   Just like her own St. John,
We'll dwell in Mary's dwelling,
   And think she's looking on.

We'll fancy that we're living
   In Joseph's lowly cot,
Of all the world the grandest,
   Though Cæsar owns it not—
The old man toiling gladly
   For Him and her from dawn,
And Jesus waiting, waiting,
   And Mary looking on.

Thus let us keep a picture
   Of Mary in our heart,
And from her holy presence
   Let us never, never part.

Her smile is far the kindest
  That e'er from kind heart shone,
And it glads one's heart to murmur,
  " My Mother's looking on."

And, oh! when all is over,
  Or all begins at last—
When earth's poor joys and troubles
  Are a dim speck in the past:
In the glory of God's palace
  May we the white robe don,
And praise the Son for ever,
  The Mother looking on.

OUR LADY'S LAMP.

NIGHT is hardly past, the chill dawn brightens,
  Duty's long day begins its dull routine—
But a mother's smile makes light the burden,
  For Mary is our Mother and our Queen.
Happy is the maiden who at rising hastens
  Down in the silence, where the dim stars shine,
On through the darkness fleeing from her taper,*
  To light the lamp before Our Lady's shrine.

* At least it was in the depth of winter-time that a certain Irish *Enfant de Marie* informed her *chère Maman*, in a letter home from school: "Je me lève à six heures, et, aussitôt habillée, je vais allumer la lampe devant l'autel de la Sainte Vierge."

Ay, be it only in her heart she lights it,
    Or like a little maiden that I know,
Boasting that hers is the duty and the honour
    First to Our Lady's altar-lamp to go.
First of her schoolmates, eagerly she rises—
    "Sweetest of duties, dear Mother, it is mine"—
(Thus to pious mother writes the pious maiden)—
    "To light the lamp before Our Lady's shrine."

So in holy convents, where gay children cluster
    Round the childlike Angels that guard them well;
So in holy convents, more tranquil, where *these* only
    Live their life of prayer in choir and cell;
So in holy homesteads, *in* the world, not *of* it,
    Peaceful homes and pure, kind friend, like thine—
May we all, at least in heart, keep burning
    The lamp of love before Our Lady's shrine.

ROSARY RHYMES.*

In the name of Father and of Son
And Holy Ghost, God Three in One,
And, Mary, for the love of thee,
We say the holy Rosary.

I.—The Joyful Mysteries.

1.—*The Annunciation.*

"Hail, full of grace! The Holy One,
The Son of God, shall be thy Son."
Low spake the handmaid of the Lord:
"Be it according to Thy word!"

---

* Some of the Indulgences granted to the Rosary require meditation on the mysteries. Many are in the habit of mentioning in each "Hail Mary" the mystery commemorated in each decade, thus: "Blessed is the fruit of thy womb, Jesus, who was crowned with thorns, &c." This breaks too much the flow of the "Hail Marys," and might at most be confined to the first "Hail Mary" of each decade. The announcement of the mysteries as given in prayer-books may readily be learned by heart. The following verses may be of use to some for this purpose.

It is easy to keep in mind that the Joyful, Sorrowful, and Glorious Mysteries are assigned in this same order to the first three days of each week and then to the last three, so that the Joyful Mysteries are thought of while saying the beads on Monday and Thursday, the Sorrowful on Tuesday and Friday, the Glorious on Wednesday and Saturday. As for the Sundays, the season of the year determines which of the three sets of mysteries is appropriate: after Christmas, the Nativity and other Joyful Mysteries; after Easter, the Resurrection and other Glorious Mysteries; in the penitential times of Lent and Advent, the Sorrowful Mysteries.

2.—*The Visitation.*

O'er the bleak hills in March she sped,
Comfort and grace around to shed.
"God's Mother cometh thus to me!
Blest amongst women shalt thou be."

3.—*The Nativity.*

Glory to God on high! for low
Hath He stooped down to heal our woe.
Glory to Christ our Lord for aye,
Who shivering in the manger lay.

4.—*The Presentation.*

Clasp Him, old Simeon, to thy breast,
Then ask of God to let thee rest.
But, ah! hast thou no gentler word
For that young Mother than the sword?

5.—*The Finding in the Temple.*

He's lost! to those fond hearts what pain!
He's lost—but joy! He's found again.
"We've sought for Thee with tears, my Son!"
"My Father's work must needs be done."

II.—The Sorrowful Mysteries.

1.—*The Agony in the Garden.*

Crushed down, O Jesus, 'neath my sins,
Thy Heart Its agony begins.
"Father, thy will, not mine, be done!"
Thou prayest, as the red streams run.

2.—*The Scourging.*

Shudder, my soul, with grief and awe,
As if ear heard, as if eye saw,
How, thick as hail, the lashes fell
On Him, "who hath done all things well."

3.—*The Crowning with Thorns.*

Unmoved shall I behold thy woe,
Because endured so long ago?
Thou lovest me as truly now
As when the rude thorns rent Thy brow.

4.—*The Carrying of the Cross.*

While up the Mount his Cross He bore,
His Mother tracked Him by his gore,
Till, tottering 'neath the weight, He fell—
That Mother's anguish who could tell?

5.—*The Crucifixion.*

Nailed to the cruel, shameful Tree
For three long hours, thy Saviour see.
Go, stand with Mary near the Cross,
Nor shrink from shame, or pain, or loss.

III.—THE GLORIOUS MYSTERIES.

1.—*The Resurrection.*

The gloom hath passed from earth away,—
Arise, O Sun! whose smile is day.
He who was dead hath eager flown
To where his Mother mourneth lone.

2.—*The Ascension.*

The pageant fadeth up from sight;
The gazers, tranced in meek delight,
Hear white-robed angels chide their pain:
"He who is gone will come again."

3.—*The Descent of the Holy Ghost.*

With patient longings deep, serene,
The Twelve are waiting with their Queen,
Till God fulfil their souls' desire—
And see! they flash, those tongues of fire.

4.—*The Assumption.*

Say who is she who upward soars,
Leaning on Him her soul adores?
The King of heaven has whispered, "Come!"
And bids his Mother welcome home.

5.—*The Coronation.*

Joy in the courts of Sion! Bow,
Saints, angels! as on Mary's brow
Gleams bright yon crown of dazzling sheen,
And heaven exultant greets its Queen.

* * *

The blessed beads are numbered all;
"Hail, holy Queen!" on thee we call
To hallow all our pilgrim days
Into a rosary of praise.

THE STORY OF MATER ADMIRABILIS.*

In the Convent of the Trinità
   De' Monti, in old Rome,
Our Lady's month of flower and song,
   Green leaves, blue skies, had come;
And joy was in the sunny air,
   And in the garden bowers,
And joy was in the hearts of all
   The little birds and flowers.
But May-time true can only be
   For those to whom the May
Is dear for Mary's own dear sake:
   And such, in sooth, were they,
Who five-and-twenty years ago
   Had made their happy home
In the Convent of the Trinità
   De' Monti, in old Rome.
'Twas May, and round Our Lady's shrine
   They gathered fondly there,
Those Spouses of the Sacred Heart,
   With wreath, and hymn, and prayer.

---

* Father Alfred Monnin, who was a fellow-worker with the Venerable John Baptist Vianney, Curé d'Ars, and who wrote his biography in a manner almost worthy of the subject, has written also a very attractive volume on the devotion to the *Mater Admirabilis*, of which a translation has been published at New York. Père Monnin is now a member of the Society of Jesus.

They mused on all the loveliness
    Of every changing phase
In Mary's hidden life of love,
    And work, and prayer, and praise—
"*Hidden the most with Christ in God,*"*
    Ere yet the Christ had come,
Whilst in the temple Mary found
    Her holy childhood's home.

This child-like aspect of our Queen,
    Far more than all the rest,
Touched one amid that virgin band
    And all her soul possessed,
Until in contemplation deep
    The tender vision grew
A living picture which she fain
    Would beckon all to view.
She longs before the eyes of all
    To make that vision start
Of the little maiden first of all
    To choose the better part.
And soon her pious wish is gained—
    "Along this corridor,
Dear sister, many feet shall pace,
    As many paced before:

† Colosa. iii. 3.

Bid these mute walls discourse of Her
  Whose daughters fond are we,
That, looking up, our eyes may smile
  Our Mother's face to see."

Then Sister Pauline for her task
  With eager joy prepares—
No scene that pen inspired hath drawn,
  Or pencil rare, she dares,
But the little maiden, Mary,
  In the sacred precincts hiding,
And through her rounds of work and prayer
  With meek perfection gliding,
Ere yet Archangel's pinion thrilled
  Her chamber's lonely calm,
Ere yet the name of "Mother" fell
  From Jesus' lips like balm—
While she is still in tenderest bloom,
  A lowly Hebrew maid,
Lurking within the cool repose
  Of the sanctuary's shade.
Alone in holy thought she sits,
  But not with idle hands—
Touching her modest mantle's hem
  Her busy distaff stands.
Her open book is fondly laid
  Within the basket neat,

Which holds material for her toil,
    On the pavement at her feet.
On her right hand a lily droops
    Its chalice pure and pale,
Towards Her, the passion-flower of God,
    The lily of the vale.
An aureole rims her hooded brow,
    Her eyes are downward bent;
Her heart?—ah! all its burning sighs
    Are upward, heavenward sent.
And all her outer semblance
    Is cheerful prayer and toil,
And in her soul a purity
    No breath can ever soil.
And this is she on whom the gaze
    Of the Eternal Three
Is riveted with boundless love,
    From all eternity.
She with a Mother's sacred sway
    The Omnipotent shall rule—
The *Mater Admirabilis*
    Of Him, the Wonderful.*

The Sister Pauline's task is done.
    Ah! many a happy tear
From the holy and the sinful
    Shall steal forth silent here;

---

* "His name shall be called Wonderful."—*Isaias*, ix. 6.

THE STORY OF MATER ADMIRABILIS.

And many a knee shall bend in faith,
  And many a lip shall say:
" *O Mater Admirabilis !*
  Ora, ora pro me."

Such is the name we give to her,
  Though softer idioms choose
Madonnina del Giglio,
  La Sainte petite Fileuse,
With other names more sweet and fond
  That can be said or sung
By uninspired lips like these
  In this cold Saxon tongue.
But, if our lips could, like our hearts,
  In Celtic accents pray,
Ah! what a liquid gush of song
  Would well up here to-day,
For Her the Child Immaculate,
  In the holy place apart,
Best loved already by that Love
  Which soon shall own a HEART.

The twentieth of October's suns
  Shone on the Pincian Hill,
Just four-and-twenty years ago.*
  What crowds unwonted fill

---

* Hence the day fixed for the Festival.

The Convent of the Sacred Heart!
  A heart most like that Heart
Has come, its saintly benison
  As Father to impart.
Great Pio Nono's pontiff-soul
  Before that fresco prays:
"A pious thought to paint our Queen
  In those young years," he says,
"When she might almost seem to be
  Forgotten by us all."—
Forgot no longer! Not in vain
  His lightest word may fall.
That twentieth of October's suns
  Each after-year has seen
Our *Mater Admirabilis*,
  Our little child-like Queen,
Honoured and blessed and glorified
  In loving filial ways,
With holy Mass and festal rite
  And songs of grateful praise,
In that Convent of the Trinità
  De' Monti, in old Rome,
And in all its sister convents,
  Like this dear convent-home:
And the pious fresco, multiplied
  A thousand, million fold,
By chisel, pencil, dye, and brush,
  Its tale of love has told

To countless hearts in every nook
  Of Mary's wide domain,
Spreading by gentlest sympathies
  Her Son's dear-purchased reign.
And many a gracious miracle
  Within the senses' ken,
And many seen but by the Eye
  That reads the hearts of men;
And many a term of penal fire
  Spared to the souls forgiven;
And many a ray of glory earned
  For many a brow in heaven;
And many a pure and holy thought,
  And many a contrite tear,
And many a vain allurement scorned,
  And many a vanquished fear;
And many a sorrow, small or great,
  Endured with patient smile;
And many a generous victory
  O'er tempter's subtlest wile;
And many a turning from earth's joys
  Unto the joy divine—
O Mater Admirabilis!
  These blessed works are *thine*.

But we!—ah, yes, not only warm
  Beneath Her mantle here,*

---

* Written for the pupils of an Irish Convent of the Sacred Heart.

But wheresoe'er be cast our lot,
    Our Mother's always near;
And from the thickest press of life
    Our souls shall steal apart
To our *Mater Admirabilis,*
    And Thee, O Sacred Heart!
Our hours shall be with *Aves* strewn,
    And still each heart shall pray:
" *O Mater Admirabilis!*
    Ora, ora pro me."

OUR LADY'S OFFICE AT MATINS.

(Quem terra, pontus, sidera, etc.)

Whom earth, and sea, and skies
  Obey, adore, declare—
Who rules the world with order wise
  Doth Mary's bosom bear.

Whom sun, and moon, and all
  Serve in their time and place—
While heavenly graces round her fall
  The Maiden doth embrace.

Oh, Mother, blest and fair!
  The Lord supreme who holds
Within his hand the worlds of air
  Thy virgin womb enfolds.

Blest with God's message sweet,
  Thou through the Spirit hast
That Fruit in Whom the nations greet
  Their Long-desired at last.

Glory, O Lord, to Thee,
  The Virgin's virgin Son!
To Father and to Spirit be
  Glory while ages run!

TO THE SACRED HEART.*

O Heart of Jesus, purest Heart!
Altar of holiness thou art,
Cleanse my foul heart, so hard and cold,
And stained by sins so manifold.

Take from me, Lord, this tepid will,
Which doth thy Heart with loathing fill;
And then infuse a spirit new,
A fervent spirit, deep and true.

Most humble heart of all that beat,
Heart full of goodness, meek and sweet!
Give me a heart more like to thine,
And light the flame of love in mine.

But, ah! were ev'n my heart on fire
With all the seraphim's desire,
Till love a conflagration proved—
Not yet wouldst thou enough be loved.

That therefore thou may'st worthily
Be loved, O loving Lord, by me,
That love which in thy Heart doth burn
Give me, to love Thee in return.

* Original in Appendix.

May this thy love's most fiery dart
Strike deep and set on fire my heart,
And in that burning may it be
Dissolved and utterly consumed in Thee!

Death to be sought with yearnings high,
Thus from love's violence to die!
Ah! may my heart love's victim prove
For the Redeemer's heart of love!

So let me die for love of Thee,
O Heart all full of love for me,
That with a new heart's virgin hoard
I may begin to love Thee, Lord!

DANTE'S PRAYER TO THE BLESSED VIRGIN.*

O VIRGIN Mother, Daughter of thy Son,
Of creatures all the lowliest, loftiest one,
Term of God's counsel, fixed ere time begun.

* Vergine Madre, figlia del tuo Figlio, &c.—*Paradiso*, canto 33.

Our human race thou hast to such degree
Ennobled in thy Maker's eye that He
His creature's child hath not disdained to be.

Kindled anew within thy womb's pure shrine
Did burn the love beneath whose glow benign
Bloomed in eternal peace this Flower divine.

Here unto us art thou the noonday light
Of charity—below in earth's dark night
Thou art of hope the living fountain bright.

Lady! so great thou art, thy power so high,
Who longs for grace nor breathes to thee his sigh
Would have his wishes without wings to fly.

Thy bounty succoureth not him alone
Who asks for it, but oftentimes is known
Freely to come ere the demand hath flown.

In thee all mercy, clemency we find,
In thee all splendour—all in thee combined,
Whatever is of good in human kind.

O Queen who canst whate'er thou wilt! I pray
That he who hath such wonders seen to-day
'Neath thy protection ever safe may stay.

HYMN TO MARY IMMACULATE.*

BY THE LATE CARDINAL DE GEISSEL, ARCHBISHOP OF COLOGNE.

Virgin of virgins! thou who art
Of all the dearest to God's heart,
   Thou glorious Queen of all the blest!
To thee our fervent hymns we raise,
Salute thee, bless thee, love and praise:
   Ah! hear the prayers to thee addressed.

But who can worthy praises find
Wherewith to praise thee, Virgin kind,
   Of highest gifts thou fount and spring?
All full art thou of graces rare,
Serene and gentle and all fair,
   The tabernacle of the King.

Oh! what great things the Mighty One
Hath unto thee his handmaid done,
   Still adding richer grace to grace;
For He who ruleth earth and heaven,
To thee, below, above, hath given
   A daughter's, spouse's, mother's place.

* The original in the Appendix.

Belov'd ere yet the world was framed,
Thee before all God chose and claimed,
  And his delight in thee He made.
From sin not rescued as a prey,
But freed before in higher way—
  First-fruits of those whose price was paid

O Virgin, truly blessed! stain
Did never on thy soul remain,
  While here thou didst our exile bear.
In thy conception sinless all,
Delivered from the mighty fall
  By privilege which none may share.

While grace with nature strove for thee,
Grace claimed thee all its own to be,
  And victory remained with grace;
It kept thee pure, without, within,
From ev'n the faintest trace of sin,
  And raised thee to thy wondrous place.

Of the new law of love restored
New Eve, forechosen of the Lord,
  The consort of his glorious state:
Thou hast the furious dragon quelled,
And with victorious foot hast held
  Prostrate the fiend of hellish hate.

HYMN TO MARY IMMACULATE.

In purest white thou still hast shone,
Amid the pure thou pure alone
  O'er all the stars hast sped thy way;
O'er all the saints of every clime,
O'er all the angel-choirs sublime
  Extends the sceptre of thy sway.

Now at thy Son's right hand on high,
Thy prayer doth for his mercy cry
  Towards all the ransomed of his blood;
Gifts from thy hands pour down like rain—
Ah! for us, too, vouchsafe to gain
  The heavenly life's eternal good.

Star of the sea to us be thou,
Lest, as this world's wild waves we plough,
  We perish in the angry tide;
Through thee the Saviour has been given;
Be then for us the gate of heaven,
  Which unto life may open wide.

Kind, clement Virgin! lead, we pray,
Lead us securely on our way,
  Until life's banishment is o'er.
Defend and guard us to the last,
Bring us to see, when time is past,
  Thee and thy Son for evermore.

Teach us to pray as thou hast prayed,
To watch, to combat, undismayed,
  Whilst thy approving smile is seen;
Thy bounteous gifts upon us shower,
And ever be in suppliant power
  The Church's guardian, mother, queen!

Make us in faith to persevere,
In charity and hope sincere,
  Unstained by sin's malignant stain;
And may the flock, whose pastors now
To thee their fond allegiance vow,
  For ever 'neath thy care remain.

THE NAME OF MARY.[*]

Mary! that holy name hath scarcely died
  Upon my lips, that name immaculate,
  When my torn heart regains its placid state,
And in my eyes the tears of grief are dried.
Mary! I name Her, and a boundless tide
  Of rapture doth my bosom inundate
  With sweetness so unutterably great
That, to contain it, all its strength is tried.

[*] From an Italian sonnet, which is given in the Appendix. The author, Father Henry Nozzi, S.J., was born in 1808, and died in 1857. A volume of his *Carmina Selecta*, chiefly in a great variety of Latin metres, was published at Rome in 1863.

Mary! that name secure shall bear me on
  Amid life's perils; in that mighty name
    The menaces of fortune I defy.
And, when my term of mortal life is gone,
  In my last moment Mary's help I'll claim—
    Her name upon my lips, content I'll die.

MOTHER MOST PURE.[*]

Adjuva filium,
  O pia Parens!
Affer auxilium,
  O culpâ carens!
	Mother most tender,
	  Help thy poor child.
	Haste with thy succour,
	  Maid undefiled!

Mater amabilis,
  Et sine labe,
Mei tam labilis
  Tu curam habe.
	Amiable Mother,
	  Stainless and fair!
	Take a frail creature
	  Into thy care.

Per tot discrimina
  Serva me purum;
Ad mortis limina
  Perduc securum.
	'Mid countless perils
	  Still keep me pure;
	On through death's portal
	  Lead me secure.

[*] *Messenger of the Sacred Heart*, May, 1879.

Quocumque gentium
    Ire jubetur,
Terram viventium
    Ingredi detur!

Amabilissima,
    Post mille dona
Mea novissima
    Tu spe corona.

Tu me certato
    Bono certamine,
Et consummato
    (Tuo juvamine)

Vitæ curriculo,
    Fide servata,
Duc e periculo,
    Mater amata!

Where'er my fortune
    Here may be cast,
The land of the living
    Mine be at last!

Thou, O most loving!
    Dost thy gifts shower:
With hope unfailing
    Crown my last hour.

When I the battle
    Have fought and won,
And 'neath thy guidance
    Life's course is run;

When, living, dying,
    My faith I've proved,
Take me from danger,
    Mother beloved!

ST. JOSEPH, OUR FATHER.

O FATHER of my Lord! most near and dear
    To those whom I would fain hold nearest, dearest,—
My love is growing all too bold, I fear,
    So kind and fatherly the face thou wearest.
Yet, great St. Joseph! let me, let me call thee
Father, and in a father's rights instal thee.

For thou wast father unto Him who said,
    And bade us say unto the Same, *Our Father!*
And e'en as one, whose hour of life is sped,
    Will his loved kindred round his pillow gather;
So did thy Son, our Elder Brother, measure
His failing breath to leave to us his treasure.

He from his dying couch (a hard one!) spake
    To John and us: "Behold, behold your Mother!"
Nay, like thy namesake, when we guilty quake,
    "Fear not," He whispers, "am not I your Brother?"
Thus, Joseph, art thou father to our Brother,
O spouse of Mary! husband of our Mother!

Saint, envied most of all the saints in heaven,
    Highest (save One) of all beneath divine,
To thee, in sooth, most blessed lot was given—
    What heaven has best, on earth was wholly thine.
Thy head was laid on Jesus' breast when dying,
And Mary hung above thee, mutely sighing.

Ah! by the sadness of that happy hour,
  Haste to my aid when my last hour is come;
Patron of Death! prove then thy sovereign power—
  Bring me to her—to Him—oh! bring me home.
Thy smile and hers will soothe my soul's misgiving,
When He, thy foster-child, shall judge the dead and
  living.

SONNET TO ST. JOSEPH.

Saints know thee best, oh, hidden, silent saint!
  And would that I could feel a little part
  Of that great love Theresa's kindred heart
Felt for thee, Foster-father! But the taint,
The chill, is on my soul; and few and faint
  The prayers that from this earthly bosom dart
  Up to that heavenly throne whereon thou art
In glory, not too high to hear my plaint.

Patron of all who work in humble ways!
  Pray that from pure and earnest motive I
    May fill with patient toil the moments flying;
Patron of happy death-beds! when my days
  Have reached their term, be thou, dear Joseph! nigh,
    With Mary and with Jesus, while I'm dying.

THE JOYS AND SORROWS OF ST. JOSEPH.*

Mighty Joseph, son of David!
   High and glorious is thy state—
Of our Lord the Foster-father,
   Mary's spouse immaculate.
The Almighty's faithful servant,
   Of the Holy Family
Head and father. Oh! I pray thee,
   Be a father unto me.

Sorely was thy bosom troubled
   Till the mystery was revealed
Which the Lord had wrought in Mary
   Who in patience all concealed.
But an angel soon from heaven
   Bids thy loving doubts to cease;
So may every care and trial
   Turn for me to joy and peace.

With the Virgin young and tender,
   In the winter-time forlorn,
Thou to Bethlehem didst journey
   That our Lord might there be born.

---

* From the *Officium Parvum Sancti Joseph.*

As thy God thou didst adore Him,
   While He in the manger lay;
Now is He in heaven exalted—
   Turn to Him for us and pray!

Flying at the angel's warning,
   Far from Herod's fury wild,
Long in Egypt didst thou tarry
   With the Virgin and the Child.
By thy toil, thy pain, thy sadness,
   In that exile dark and drear,
Help me in the cares and sorrows
   Which may be my portion here.

Home from Egypt's land returning,
   Thou wouldst rest in Galilee,
But to Nazareth art bidden,
   That the Child secure may be.
Souls retiring, sweet, and humble,
   Thou dost still for Jesus seek:
That my heart may be his garden,
   Make it humble, pure, and meek.

Thou didst search, with loving anguish,
   For the little Jesus lost;
But, in finding Him, what rapture
   Purchased at that sorrow's cost!

Thee, my light, my life, my Jesus,
  May I never lose by sin!
May my heart be pure and simple,
  So that thou may'st rest therein!

Jesus, Mary, hung above thee
  On that sad yet happy day
When, with their fond arms around thee,
  Passed thy gentle soul away.
Oh! when death shall come to take me,
  All its terrors I'll defy,
If, with Jesus and with Mary,
  Thou, dear Joseph, wilt be nigh.

Thus, O glorious Saint, my homage
  I thy grateful client pay.
Hear my prayer and smile upon me,
  Guide and guard me on my way.
May I 'neath thy kind protection
  Safely reach my journey's close,
And with thee, in heaven's bright palace,
  Through eternity repose!

ST. JOHN THE BAPTIST.
(*June* 24.)

WHERE Hebron nestles 'mid Judea's hills,
    They pass their tranquil days "without complaint;"*
One heart two pure and faithful bosoms fills,
    Fit parents for a Saint.

Their prime is past when to the holy pair
    A child of miracle and prayer is given,
Scarce claim they in their babe a parent's share,
    But give him all to heaven.

"And thou, O boy! shalt be of the Most High
    The prophet; thou shalt go before his face,
His paths prepare, and to his world supply
    The light of saving grace."

But who is this that o'er the hills with speed
    Bears kindly help and many a loving word?
"Ah! why doth *she* her lowly cousin heed—
    The Mother of the Lord?"

'Tis Mary's arms that fondle first the child;
    There, too, precursor of her own dear Son,
Pressed where the Saviour's Heart, so sweet and mild,
    With Mary's beats as one.

* Luke, i. 6.

But Mary leaves them soon for Bethlehem,
   For Egypt, Nazareth, and Calvary.
Nor will their son abide at home with them,
     But far from men will flee.

Into the wilderness the child has fled.
   The child? A hero in his ardour brave;
The camel raiment, the hard rock a bed,
     And food the locusts gave.

But, when the hour was come, a voice was heard,
   The voice of one in the lone desert crying.
The Baptist preached by deed as well as word,
     Precursor, too, in dying.

Great Saint, whose eulogy the lips divine
   Have spoken, saying, Greater there is none;
Prophet, Apostle, Hermit, Martyr—thine
     Are all the aureoles in one.

Austere thou art, unearthly, far removed
   From our smooth, selfish, self-indulgent day.
Ah! how our sloth is by thy zeal reproved;
     Yet pity us, and pray.

ST. MATTHEW.

(*September* 21.)

"He, not in vain, beside yon breezy lake,
Bade the meek Publican his gainful seat forsake."—KEBLE.

LEVI the Publican beside his door
  Marked some poor peasants slowly passing by;
But One amid them walked who seemed far more
  Than those rude fishermen, so grand his eye,
  With such majestic mildness raised on high—
To catch his words his comrades forward bent.
  And Levi trembled as the group drew nigh,
For a deep-searching glance was towards him sent,
And Jesus whispered soft, *Come with Me!*—and he went.

Levi that night for his new Master made
  A feast, which he with his old friends would share—
Sinners like him, yet he was not afraid,
  For He who came not for the just was there
  To lead their spirits captive unaware,
And wean from earth each earthy, selfish heart.
  Thus did that hospitable feast prepare
Some souls perchance for the Apostle's part;
And thou of such high calls, dear saint! the patron art.*

---

* The dedication of Father Faber's "Creator and Creature" runs thus:
"To St. Matthew, the apostle and evangelist of the Incarnate Word, the pattern of obedience to divine vocations, the model of prompt submission to divine inspirations, the teacher and the example of correspondence to

She heard that call, the royal Ethiop maid,
   Iphigenia, thy heroic child;
She changed her crown for one that ne'er can fade,
   And faltered not, but, meekly scornful, smiled
   When the new King, with heathen crime defiled,
Of her pure heart would rob her Spouse divine.
   Then Hirtacus, with jealous fury wild,
   Slew thee, her teacher, at the altar-shrine:
And thus a martyr's death for purity was thine.

Apostle, martyr, first evangelist—
   Like only John, yet martyr more than he;
Thy greatness, like a peak through cloud and mist,
   Looms all the vaster that we dimly see
   Less what thou art than what thou needs must be.
Chosen of God for purpose so divine,
   Divinest gifts are surely rife in thee.
And so my heart hath round thee learned to twine
Closer, the more it grows (God help me!) like to thine.

For thou hast lived too near the beating Heart
   Of Him who wept o'er Lazarus, not to yearn
In pity towards me and to take my part,
   When sinful ways would call for vengeance stern—

grace, who left all for God—self and the world and wealth—at God's one word, without question, without reserve, without delay, to be for ever in the Church the doctor, the prophet, and the patron, the comfort and the justification of those who follow heavenly calls in the world's despite, and who give themselves in love as He gave Himself, without limit or condition, as creatures to their Creator."

Yes, far too long with Jesus not to earn
  Some of his kindness for thy spirit's dower,
For oft hast thou, their lessons sweet to learn,
  Watched all his tender looks, ay, hour by hour,
And all his deeds of grace and all his words of power.

Came it from thee,* that touching trait which rests
  In fond tradition?—how that He who said,
"The foxes have their holes, the birds their nests,
  But *I* have not whereon to lay my head"—
How that, one summer's night, He made his bed
Out on the homeless heath, and round Him lay
  The wearied Twelve. And so the dark night sped,
While slept the Sleepless, He, the Light of day,
He the All-seeing slept, but rose at dawn to pray.

Perhaps 'twas thou that, waking up that night,
  Marked the kind Master steal from each to each,
As if afraid to break their slumbers light,
  With muffled tread and low-breathed, lulling speech,

---

* No, but from St. Peter. Père de Ligny, in the forty-ninth chapter of his excellent "Life of Christ," joins the incident with those words of our Lord: "I am not come to be ministered to but to minister." "What Pope St. Clement relates of his master, St. Peter, may be set down here. He says that when the holy apostle saw anyone sleeping, the tears came to his eyes. When asked the reason, he answered that this reminded him of his dear Lord, who, while they all slept, kept watch for all, and, if the covering happened to be disarranged for any of them, would settle the poor couch again without disturbing the sleeper."

And gentlest art that mother's heart doth teach,
Smoothing the pillow of her cradled pet.
   Even so low the Eternal's care doth reach,
   The slumberer's dress in warmer folds to set,
Wrapping them closer round against the night-dews wet.

If not for this, for much of written lore
   We thank thee, Matthew, pensman of the Word!
But most that thou, alone of all the Four,
   Talkest to us of Mary's spouse and lord.
   And hence the Church doth gratefully accord
The Foster-father's altar-prayer to thee—
   None higher could her liturgy afford;
Praying, as I do now, that all, which she
Fails else to gain, gained through thy prayers may be.

Take, then, this lay, by filial love inspired—
   For words of love can reach e'en to thy throne—
My loving words, how mean soe'er attired,
   On this thy Feast, dear Saint, thou'lt not disown.
   Ah, no! but when my cheerful exile's flown,
When earth's long task is done, in realms beyond
   Thou'lt smiling bid me welcome as thine own,
And I shall be, as when my first life dawned,
Thy namesake, client, child—more near, but not more fond.

ST. MARY MAGDALEN.
(*July* 22.)

"If Thou wert here, my brother had not died,"
   The mourner whispers meekly through her tears;
   But now her heart thrills with strange hopes and
      fears,
For He the Lord of life is by her side.

"And Jesus wept," and they who saw Him cried,
   "See how He loved him!" Then He spake the word
   Of power which in his tomb the dead man stirred
And through his veins poured back life's crimson tide.

Beside another tomb that mourner weeps,
   And, as her tears falls fast, the angels say,
"See how she loved Him!" Still her watch she keeps
   And murmurs—"they have taken Him away!"
But He for whom she mourns no longer sleeps—
   His night hath changed into eternal day.

ST. AGNES.

(*January* 21.)

Once there was a little maiden,
Bright with thirteen southern summers.;
Beautiful, and gay, and holy,
And the maiden's name was Agnes.

Fair of soul and fair of forehead,
Meek as snow-white, tender lambkin;
Sunny as the skies above her,
And as pure and speckless—Agnes.

Long ago, in world still heathen,
Sprang that flower and blossomed sweetly;
And the eyes that saw her loved her—
Many sought the love of Agnes.

But the child hath heard of Jesus,
Virgin Son of Virgin Mother;
Her young soul is wedded to Him,
Earthly love is nought for Agnes.

He from Heaven smiles on her fondly,
Yearns to draw her nearer, nearer;
Rarest flower of all his garden,
Gleams the modest snow-drop, Agnes.

Will she, yearning as He yearneth,
Like the snow-drop, melt serenely?
Ah! not thus died He who loves her—
Death, a hero's death, for Agnes.

For that maiden was a Roman—
In her weakness, strongest, bravest;
Virgin's truth and martyr's courage
Nerve the gentle, fawn-like Agnes.

Firm she stands before the tempter,
'Neath the tyrant's frown she pales not;
For she sees but Him who loves her,
Hears Him calling "Come, O Agnes!"

Near the throne of Him who loves her,
Crowned with red rose and white lily,
Shines the little martyr-maiden:—
Pray for us, ah! dear St. Agnes!

ST. EMERENTIANA.

(*January* 23.)

MIDWAY between the first and second feast
Of blessed Agnes, little martyr-maid,
The graceful fondness of the Church's heart,
Each opening year, recalls with love and praise
The beautiful and soothing memory
Of yet another little martyr-maid.
Agnes and Emerentiana, hail!

Their feasts come side by side, as side by side
Their lot on earth, and now in heaven their lot;
For Emerentiana of St. Agnes
Was foster-sister, playmate fond and true,
Partner in every task and sport and prayer:
Nay, not in *every* prayer: *she* could not stay
Till all the holy awful rites were done,
But with the catechumens would retire,
Hoping that soon, like Agnes, she might be
Baptised into the perfect fold of Christ.
Still unbaptised, yet Christian to the core;
And she with her dear foster-sister loved
To speak of Jesus and his Virgin Mother—
Till all their longing was to prove their love
For Him who for their love had lived and died.
Agnes and Emerentiana, hail!

But Agnes left her Emerentiana,
Left her to give her virgin life and love
To Jesus, who had whispered, "Agnes, come!"
Eager through martyr-pangs she boundeth towards
    Him,
And leaveth Emerentiana lone;
And she can only weep upon the tomb
Of her lost Agnes, out beyond the Gate
Then Nomentana called, now Gate of Agnes,
Whither already Christian pilgrims thronged
To crave the aid and bless the name of Agnes.

There found they her, the ruthless Pagan fiends
Who slew her Agnes; and her loving heart
Swelled in her bosom, and she looked at them,
And their bold, scowling eyes quailed 'neath her
    glance,
While she rebuked their impious heathendom,
And blessed aloud the ever-blessed name
Of Jesus, in whose name her Agnes died.
Again the demons rage, and, with their blades,
Rush in blind fury on the tender child.
"Bring me, O Jesus, to thyself—to Agnes!"
Thus on the grave of Agnes, martyr-maid,
Gushes another spring of virgin-blood,
And instantly, with radiant, wistful joy,
Upon her lips the name of Jesus, Agnes—
The love of Jesus, Agnes, in her heart,—

Baptisèd in her own young virgin-blood,
Above her darling foster-sister's grave
The little Emerentiana dies.
Agnes and Emerentiana, hail!

ST. DOROTHY.
(*February* 6.)*

Constantius fills the imperial throne,
    Father to Constantine,
He, too, of mildness not unmeet
    To found the Christian line.
But Diocletian's code at times
    Yet wreaks its bloody will—
As waves will toss, and foam, and fret
    After the storm is still.

Before the ruthless Governor
    Of Cappadocia stands
The high-born maiden Dorothy,
    Serene, with folded hands.
Her brow is fair, her cheek is red,
    Her laugh breaks low and clear;
And young she is and innocent—
    And wherefore stands she here?

---

* The best account of this saint to be found in English is given by Father Anderdon, S.J., in the *Irish Monthly* for February, 1880 (vol. viii., p. 71).

But here are only smiles for her,
    And counsels kindly meant;
"Blench not, fair maiden," smirks the Judge,
    "Thou art but hither sent
To check those foolish, slanderous tales
    Which link thy honoured name
With his—the Wretch of Galilee—
    Who died the death of shame."

"Who died the death of shame," she cries,
    "To save the souls He made,
And for our ransom, on the Tree
    His last red life-drop paid.
Be glory to the one true God,
    One God in Persons Three!
Be glory to the Eternal Son,
    Jesus who died for me!"

"Hold!" yells the angry Governor,
    "This impious jargon cease.
Adore the gods whom all adore,
    And live thy life in peace.
Adore or die!"—"Or die?" she saith:
    "Choose sterner threat than this,
For death is but the golden gate
    To radiant home of bliss—

That garden fair, whose autumn fruits
    'Mid flowers of springtime gleam;
Nor blight nor tempest dares to break
    The rose's summer dream.

Ah, might I fade from this dark earth,
   Melt quite away, and flee
To Him, my Lover and my Lord,
   Jesus who died for me!"

The young Theophilus o'erhears
   The martyr's raptured sighs,
And with a not ungenerous scorn,
   "O Dorothy," he cries,
"If flowers and rosy fruits are there
   In this rude season found,
Send me a few."—"I will," she saith.
   The snow was on the ground.

The girl hath braved the tyrant's rage;
   All tortures, threats, are vain.
Now butchers eager press, their steel
   In virgin blood to stain;
While at the last before her kneels
   Yon beauteous smiling child,
A basket in his tiny hands,
   With fruits and flòw'rets piled.

"Take these unto Theophilus:
   Say Dorothy hath cried
To heaven for mercy on his soul,
   Ere with glad heart she died.

Tell him I go, and he shall come
  Where flowers and fruits abound
Of softer sheen, of sunnier tint."—
  The snow was on the ground.

The snow shone white o'er all the ground,
  Save where the ruby gush
From that young fearless Christian heart
  Forced pagan earth to blush.
St. Dorothy is throned on high,
  Close, close to Christ, her Spouse;
And by her side Theophilus,
  With laurel round his brows.

ST. MONICA.

(*May* 4.)

AMONG the sainted matrons whom we honour
   With Mass and matin song,
One draws the gaze of filial love upon her
   From all the throng.
Next to St. Anne, the Blessed Virgin's mother,
I prize St. Monica o'er every other.

Great is the glory of Augustine—high
   His place on earth, in heaven.
But if St. Monica with prayer and sigh
   Less hard had striven
To bring the child forth to his truer birth,
What were his fame in heaven, and e'en on earth?

His father's name to us is nothing strange—
   "Patrick," but ah! no saint.
Saint surely she who all so soon could change
   That pagan taint—
Who wept and prayed, and suffered till she won
Her heathen husband, her half-heathen son.

Have you not seen them* sitting on the beach?
    The younger face less fair—
They talk not, 'tis society for each
    The other's there—
Hands interlaced, deep eyes upturned in thought:
Their hearts bless God, whose grace the change hath wrought.

Hid in her son, yet many a touching trace
    In Austin's page we find,
Which shows her like to him not more in face
    Than royal mind.
Another item for the common story—
How large a mother's part in hero's glory.

St. Monica, still many a mother shares
    Thy strong maternal faith,
Still sheds such bitter tears, still breathes such prayers,
    To save from death
Some soul perchance from all hearts else exiled
As vile or wicked, yet *her* child, her child!

Pray for the wretched mothers who this hour
    Weep for the doubly dead,
Weep for the cherished wanderer, and shower
    Tears on *his* head,
Whose faults and sins would weary out all others,
Save the meek heart of Jesus, or a mother's.

---

* In Ary Scheffer's well-known picture which the little photograph has spread everywhere.

When thou hadst longer been away from earth
  Than she (God rest her!) yet
Who did far more for me than give me birth,
  Whose cheek was wet
With tears less bitter (God be thanked) than thine,
Austin asked prayers for thee—and I for mine.

Be *Monicas*, oh, mothers! pray and weep,
  Send ceaseless sighs to heaven,
That ye for heaven and God secure may keep
  Whom God has given.
Love them, but save their souls at any cost—
"The child of holy tears cannot be lost."

ST. PATRICK. (*March* 17.)

(A.D. 372-464.)

On high, before the throne of God,
  Amid the saints who share
The glory and the blessedness—
  Is there no loving care
For us, who in this tearful vale
  Down far below sustain
The weary fight which they have fought,
  The crown they've gained to gain?

Ah! one dear saint forgets us not,
   But from the bliss of heaven
Yearns fondly towards that spot of earth
   To which his life was given:
Father of many children strewn
   O'er every land and wave,—
The Guardian Angel of our race,
   To cheer, and guide, and save.

He came a captive to these shores;
   But once again he came,
"A conqueror to conquer,"
   In the might of Peter's name.
And to our sires what Pontiff sent
   Of Christ the welcome tale?
The smiter of the wretch who dared
   Christ's Mother to assail!

'Twas Celestine whose voice of power
   At Ephesus proclaimed
That she, the lowly virgin, must
   "Mother of God" be named.
And while earth's bosom towards its Queen
   Thrills thus with warmer glow,
Again that voice is raised—to bless
   Our own Apostle. "Go!

"Go in the name of Mary's Son—
   Go, Patrick, forth, and bring
Yon lone green Isle beneath the sway
   Of Christ our Saviour-King.

Go forth, and wrest that race of souls
  From heathendom and hell.
Go forth!"—He went. What patrón saint
  E'er did his work so well?

He came from Rome and Celestine.
  St. Celestine is dead:
But Christ for ever lives, and now
  Reigns Leo in his stead,
Upon that throne which towers on high
  O'er falsehood, sin, and time,
Like to the marvellous dome that crowns
  St. Peter's fane sublime.

That throne is still of Christian souls
  The pilgrim-shrine, the home,
The citadel of Christendom:
  And still from sovereign Rome
The shepherds of our souls receive
  The mission Patrick sought;
For they but finish Patrick's work,
  And teach as Patrick taught.

Thus, ever since, to Irish hearts
  Unutterably dear
Each instinct of that holy Faith
  Which Patrick planted here;

Dear and more dear the Mother-maid,
  Whose Infant we adore,
And Ireland ever Catholic
  And Roman to the core.

So hath it been throughout our past,
  With all its fruitful tears.
So be it in the subtler strife
  Perchance of future years:—
The soul of Ireland fixed for aye
  In faith and patient hope,
True to God's Mother and God's Church,
  St. Patrick and the Pope.

It shall be so. Oh, grant it, God!
  By thy Almighty love,
Until the last of Celtic race
  Hath joined his kin above—
Last of the myriad souls elect
  To Patrick's bosom given:
On earth our father, father still
  Before God's throne in heaven.

BLESSED IMELDA.*

(September 16.)

"Poor little Imelda, why dost thou weep?"
She strives through her sobbing to answer: "They keep,
They keep me from Jesus! There's Agnes and Kate,
And my cousins are ready—Imelda must wait.

"'Poor Imelda must wait,' said my nun yesterday—
The nun at whose girdle I best love to play—
Even she who is always so kind, oh! so kind,
'You must wait, poor Imelda'—the tears made me blind!

"For you know I'd been hoping; ay, ever so long;
And I thought that my Saviour—perhaps it is wrong
To think so—but sure He would not turn away
If they let me creep close to his altar to-day.

---

* The story of this amiable little martyr of First Communion (who was more than seven years old) is told more fully in two holy and beautiful volumes of verse, *Songs in the Night*, by the last and best biographer of St. Catherine of Sienna, and *Voices from the Heart*, by Sister Mary Alphonsus (Ellen Downing).

"There they kneel in white dresses, so happy, so
    good—
In their hands waxen tapers are burning. Ah! would
That I, too, were kneeling among them,—but, no;
Imelda's too young and too foolish to go.

" Alas! I'm too young; cousin Mary's eleven,
And my mother has told me I'll only be seven
Next birthday. Yet, Jesus, sweet Jesus, you'll smile
On your little Imelda, and love her the while."

So she kneels in a corner, away from the crowd
Of girls in white dresses, and prays half aloud:
" Oh! come to me, Jesus, most loving, most dear;
Come nearer, come nearer, thy poor child is here."

He comes. On the altar the priest turneth round,
The little hearts flutter, the warning-bells sound.
Ecce Agnus! What meaneth that flash through
    the aisle?
Poor little Imelda, why dost thou smile?

The priest's hand is empty. Above the child glows
A star of flame. Towards it the trembling priest goes.
Whom Imelda so yearned for has pitied her sighs,
And happy tears gleam in her dark, wistful eyes.

The lover of children her youth has forgiven,
She faints in her joy. Is this death? It is heaven.
To her nest on high soareth the innocent dove,
In her first, last communion, thus dying of love.

'Mid the youngest whose glory streams down on
    our sight,
From the home where she sparkles with love and
    with light;
Robed in white, with white lilies less white than
    her brow—
Dear little Imelda will pray for us now.

ST. THOMAS AQUINAS. (*March* 7.)
[A.D. 1226-1274.]

OH! great Aquinas! high thy forehead raises
    Its ample dome the cherubim among;
Yet earth but seldom deigns to hymn thy praises,
    Nor ever Irish heart with English tongue.

And wherefore now a tribute to thy glory?
    I love all saints, yet sing not every one.
Why is this breast so drawn unto the story
    Of glorious Dominic's more glorious son?

Another father claims my soul's allegiance
    Who came for thine three centuries too late:
Yet doth he bid us in the lofty regions
    Where thou art lord, thy rule to venerate.

Thou, too, the patron art of sacred science,
    And all condemned to pour o'er musty tomes
Must learn of thee to set their last reliance
    On the meek wisdom from on high that comes.

With gentler memories love's tide is swollen—
    If soul so scant may hold a swelling tide!—
By one dear sister hath thy name been stolen
    To mark her as the Bridegroom's happy bride.

Another, born upon thy feast, or near it,
   Hath from the cradle glowed with love divine
For thee and for thy Eucharistic spirit,
   Whereof, through hers, a spark hath kindled mine.

Thus have I learned with tenderest love to love thee,
   Yet more for thine own wondrous works and words;
Apostles, martyrs, may not rank above thee—
   More wasting toils thy bookworm life affords.

Ne'er hast thou trod the scaffold of the Neros,
   In penal exile never didst thou pine;
Yet in the bead-roll of the Church's heroes
   Gleams there no grander, loftier name than thine.

Interpreter of each most darksome mystery,
   Subtlest of thinkers earth shall ever see!
E'en the glib pensman of the world's bad history,
   The learned sceptic, dares not sneer at thee.

Singer of sweetest songs* that haunt the altars
   Where our dear Pelican by stealth abides!
Our love grown cold, our faith that pines and falters,
   Each fiery word which thou hast left us, chides.

---

* Amongst others, the magnificent *Lauda Sion*, the *Verbum Supernum*, and the *Adoro te devote*. In the last occurs the epithet alluded to in the next line—*Pie Pellicane, Jesu Domine!*—which may be explained by these words from one of Moore's Melodies:—

  "Our hearts, like the young of the desert-bird's nest,
    Drink love in each life-drop that flows from thy breast."

Oh, fifth Evangelist of holy learning!
 To John in Patmos mandate gave the Lord,
"Write!" But more blessed thou this tribute earning:
 "Well hast thou written, Thomas—what reward?"

Be ours thine answer when the choice is given,
 Were wealth and fame but waiting for a nod:
"Ah! we have little wrought, have feebly striven—
 For all no guerdon save thyself, O God!"

ST. FRANCIS OF ASSISI. (*October* 4.)
[A.D. 1182-1226.]

St. Francis of Assisi, the seraph-saint of love,
Christ's glorious *poverello*, fixed all his hopes above.
He cared not for the sorrows or the shame and pain of life,
And of his wounds he recked not in the ardour of the strife.
"My God, my all!" he murmured, and yearned for nought beside;
He lived on love of Jesus, and 'twas of love he died.

His heart was large and tender, he loved the beasts and birds;
His twittering sister-swallows listened silent to his words.

The cruel wolf of Gobbio his gentle glance could
    tame,
And to his whispered bidding obedient it became.
Before the murderous brigand with prayers and
    tears he fell—
"On thine own soul have mercy!"—and he saved
    that soul from hell.

St. Francis of Assisi is glorious now in heaven,
And e'en on earth has genius its richest tribute
    given
To him the poor and lowly who only loved the cross,
And looked on wealth and honour as foolishness and
    dross.
Brave warriors, bright maidens, soon dead, forgot-
    ten long—
But Francis still is living in our hearts and in our
    song.

On the snowy heights of Dante thou, Francis, hast
    thy place;
Thy *Fioretti* charm us with subtlest, rarest grace.
The pathos of thy story the poet's soul has fired,
The highest flights of Bossuet have been by thee
    inspired;
And Giotto, Perugino, have laid in homage meet
Their art's divinest treasures beneath thy piercèd
    feet.

But gentle Father Francis will bid us link his name
With those who in his footsteps to the Heart of Jesus came—
Good Brother Giles, and Bernard, the first to join the Saint,
And Juniper, and Leo, so holy and so quaint,
And all the thousand thousands who have fasted, preached, and prayed
In the brown Franciscan habit—ne'er may its glory fade!

Great Saint! on earth thou madest meek Poverty thy bride,
And on the cross with Jesus thy flesh was crucified.
May I, in coward's measure, partake thy blissful pain,
That somewhere in Christ's kingdom I too at length may reign!
To think of thee, St. Francis, is both a joy and fear,
For *I* must win that heaven which cost *thee* not too dear.

ST. FRANCIS DE SALES. (*January* 29.)
[A. D. 1567-1627.]

His feast is come—the meek, the strong,
   The eloquent and genial saint·
Who toiled for souls so well, so long,
   And warmed the cold and cheered the faint.

His were all virtues. Burning zeal
   By patient wisdom checked and taught;
A hand to help, a heart to feel—
   True charity in word, deed, thought.

Genius was his. His voice had power
   O'er the proud great ones of his time.
Grim Unbelief and Doubt would cower
   Before his intellect sublime.

And still his words our hearts delight—
   His massive thought, his fancy's play,
His diction clear, and fresh, and bright,
   Tender, serene, and gravely gay.

We love him as a father still,
   A holy bishop like our own.
We've read his books and letters, till
   He seems like one we've seen and known.

And now his feast is come, and here
    Into glad prayers and smiles we break.
Though for his sake the day is dear,
    'Tis dearer for another's sake.

It is our mother's festal day,
    And filial, grateful hearts like ours
Wonder that 'neath its welcome ray
    E'en winter bursts not forth in flowers.

For flowers she'll take these buds of song—
    For roses, Rosaries—kind thoughts
That now within our bosoms throng,
    Hail Marys and forget-me-nots.

Her feast-day comes in winter-time:
    And, like her patron's marvellous toils,
Hers, too, lie 'mid the wintry clime
    Where heresy has gathered spoils.

But heresy and languid faith,
    And faith unwarmed by charity,
Impatient pain, unhopeful death—
    These yield to such as he and she.

She bears his name, she plays his part;
    What he has writ she acts it out,
Teaching God's love to many a heart,
    And guiding souls in life devout.*

---

* The best known of the writings of St. Francis are his "Treatise on the Love of God," and his "Introduction to a Devout Life." This piece was written for a Convent of Mercy in the north of Ireland, presided over by one whose patron is St. Francis de Sales.

ST. FRANCIS DE SALES.

Fitly his name she bears: for he
   Had dared the first to wish and plan
Sisters of Mercy, "bond yet free,"
   To tend the sick and work for man;

Therefore did he his daughters place
   Beneath the Visitation's shade.
Such was Jane Frances for a space,
   Until their purpose was gainsayed.

Not yet God willed it. 'Francis' Nuns
   Within their holy cloister lurk; .
But we (poor, feeble, helpless ones!)
   Must in our way do Francis' work.

Long may *she* help us with her care,
   Whose joyful feast we keep to-day.
God's dearest blessings may she share
   Here and hereafter! So we pray.

TO ST. IGNATIUS LOYOLA (*July* 31)
FOUNDER OF THE SOCIETY OF JESUS.
[A. D. 1491-1556.]

So many a tribute of homage and love
To patrons and friends 'mid the blessed above,
And none to my Father! Forgive me, great saint,
That never—for words are so feeble and faint—
No, never before have I striven to tell
What you and the God of my heart know full well:
The filial devotion which burns in this breast
For founder and father the wisest and best.

Dear Father Ignatius, I wish I could feel
That fervour of faith and that ardour of zeal
You felt in your worst, unregenerate days.
I almost am tempted to envy and praise
What seems to be laid to *your* charge as a sin:
The doubt which, your rough soldier-days, you were in
If chivalry did not compel you to smite
The Moor who once dared in your presence to slight
The virginal honour of Mary our Queen—
That blow no ungenerous crime would have been.

TO ST. IGNATIUS LOYOLA.

Brave soldier of Spain, braver soldier of God!
How hard and how rugged the pathway you trod.
Manresa seems easy compared with the school
Where you in ripe manhood became like a fool,
Rehearsing your grammar with children once more.
Your voyage to Palestine's mystical shore
Was less than the journey to class day by day—
But *that*, St. Ignatius, was always *your* way:
To use the means fittest for gaining your end,
While begging of God special succour to lend—
To shrink from no labour or danger or care,
To work as if nothing depended on prayer,
And then, as if all with God's clemency lay,
Most earnestly, constantly, humbly to pray.*

How grand must your nature have been, and your heart,
So deep and enduring a stamp to impart
To Xavier and hundreds of heroes since then.
You truly are one of the leaders of men;
You lead them to God. Oh! the dupe and the knave
Who at you and your children carp, snarl, and rave,
They know you not, Father Ignatius! but I
Know well you and yours, and full gladly would die

* These three lines are one of St. Ignatius' maxims versified.

Your honour and theirs to attest. Cruel shame,
That not the bad only should slander and blame
The Company banded by Captain so great!
Let Heresy give them the praise of its hate;
Let sensual, proud unbelievers detest—
The demons of hell know their enemies best—
But ye who love Jesus, rejoicing applaud
All, all who are striving to win unto God
The souls Jesus died for.
      When earth's war is done,
Ignatius, what captive hosts *you* shall have won!
Great Xavier's magnificent soul your first spoil.
And so all the marvellous fruits of his toil;
And all who your flag to the end shall uphold—
Canisius, Alphonsus, the laybrother old;
The three youthful saints to the youthful so dear;*
De Britto and Suarez, unlike in their sphere;
Francis Regis at home drawing thousands to God,
And Claver, apostle of negroes abroad;
De Lugo and Bellarmine, who teachers teach,
With Segneri, Bourdaloue, mighty in speech;
And Southwell, true poet, true martyr; St. Jure,
Rodriguez, ascetics large-minded and sure;
With all who your wise, gentle spirit and rule
Have followed in pulpit, confessional, school;

---

* St. Stanislaus Kostka, St. Aloysius Gonzaga, and Blessed John Berchmans.

And all who have striven to sanctify men
By prayer and example, the voice and the pen;
And all who have laboured and labour unknown,
And thus shall toil on till the last trump has blown:
In all that each one of your children endures,
A share shall for ever, Ignatius, be yours.

Ignatius, a saint ere your earliest vow,
A hero, an angel—what must you be now?
How vile seemed the earth when you looked up to
    heaven!*
To God and his glory your grand soul was given;
God's glory alone was your joy and your pride,
" For God's greater glory" you lived and you died.

Oh, great St. Ignatius, look down from your throne,
And do not the least of your children disown;
Pray, pray for us unto the Father of all,
Through whom and in whom you our father we
    call.
And we—may we each, in our place and our day,
Work for God while obedience guides safely our
    way;
May each to each duty, how humble soe'er,
Give soul and sense wholly, with faith and with
    prayer;

---

* Quam sordet terra dum cœlum aspicio.

May each, to your war-cry* unflinchingly true,
Live and die as the son of such father should do;
And be it to all—yes, to all of us—given
To meet as your children, Ignatius, in heaven.

ST. ALOYSIUS GONZAGA. (*June* 21.)
[A. D. 1568-1591.]

O ALOYSIUS, dear young saint!
   Help at thy hands I come to claim;
It cheers me, when my soul is faint,
   To think of thee, to name thy name.
I yearn to thee as to a brother,
   A brother gone to God before—
I love thee next to Mary Mother
   In Him whom she and thou adore.
I love but Him and her above thee,
And more thou wouldst not let me love thee.

The hoary Saints of mien austere,
   Rapt eye and venerable form,
We think of them with reverent fear—
   They cannot win a love so warm

* *Ad majorem Dei gloriam.*

ST. ALOYSIUS GONZAGA.

As thou with thine unwrinkled brow,
    Thy youthful heart and youthful face,
That smile that gleams upon me now,
    And all thy noble modest grace.
For ah! too quickly home thou hasted—
Thy twenty twelvemonths were not wasted.*

Thy sun went down before its noon,
    That should have lit up noon and even—
A few short hours it shone, but soon
    Its mild light faded from our heaven.
The ripe fruit could not keep its hold;
    Its rich load snapped the bough in twain—
God would not wait till thou grew old,
    To clasp thee to his breast again.
So, young yet old, in sainthood hoary,
Closed, high-born angel! thy brief story.

And here is one who fondly bears
    Deep in his heart thy sacred name,
And wears the habit that he wears
    Partly that thou hast worn the same:
Brother to little Stanislaus,
    Ignatius' child as thou and he—
Oh! by the love such kinship draws,
    Act a true brother's part to me.
Though sins on sins unworthy prove me,
Dear Aloysius! try and love me.

* St. Aloysius died at early dawn of June 21, 1591, aged twenty-three years, three months, and eleven days.

I pray as thou thyself hast prayed,
  While thou didst linger here below;
And, as the saints then lent thee aid,
  Thou'lt help me in thy turn, I know.
Ah! help me, help me in my need—
  Help me to work, to love, to pray—
Help me! I need thy help indeed:
  Turn not thy sweet young face away.
Turn not away thy face, dear Lewis,
But turn it, beaming kindly, to us.

TO ST. STANISLAUS KOSTKA. (*Nov.* 13.)
[A. D. 1550-1568.]

Yes, let me dare the love to say
  That's throbbing for thee in this heart,
For dearer and more dear each day,
  Sweet little Stanislaus, thou art.

So amiable art thou and mild,
  Guileless and gay and kind to all,
The youngest and the fairest child
  Of him whom I too Father call.

Brother! But *that* name points to thee
  Tortured for years without complaint.
Ah! how had Paul the heart to be
  So cruel towards his little saint?

TO ST. STANISLAUS KOSTKA.

Of princely birth, of graceful form,
   With winning manners, talents rare,
High-swelling hopes, affections warm—
   What from the world thy soul can tear?

To thy sick-couch doth Mary bring
   The healing grace—then lends to thee
To fondle in thy arms the King
   Whose knight she bids thee live to be.

Twice, too, that loving Lord, unknown
   E'en in his Eucharistic guise,
Nor borne by priestly hand, has flown
   To hush thy pining amorous sighs.

And years before, his Name o'er thee
   Gleamed on the Polish mother's breast—
For God would mark thee his, as we
   Some favourite book, with name and crest.

And so, brave boy! on fire with love
   For Him who claimed thee thus ere birth,
Since thou not yet may'st flee above,
   Thou seek'st his Brotherhood on earth.

And after weary toils and care,
   At sainted Borgia's feet thou prayest
To be of those who meekly bear
   The Name of names—and there thou stayest.

Thus, Kostka, oped thine eighteenth year:
  A novice then nine months at Rome,
Dear to all hearts—to God, so dear
  He bade thy Mother call thee home.

At dawn of her own parting-day,
  As thou hadst prayed and prophesied,
Thy happy spirit broke away,
  Dying of love as she had died.

Oh, sweetest, loveliest saint in heaven!
  Forgive love's tone, too free and wild.
To children childish names are given,
  And thou art such—God's darling child.

Angel of God! We sometimes dare
  To call thee so—and well we may,
For angels could not be more fair,
  And thou art pure and bright as they.

Angel in death, in life, in birth—
  Angel in form, in heart, in tongue—
Oh! God be blessed for blessing earth
  With saint so gentle, fair, and young!

BLESSED JOHN BERCHMANS, S.J. (*Aug.* 13.)
[A.D. 1599–1621.]

"Cum his tribus libenter moriar."

"GIVE me my rule, my cross, my beads,
    With these three gladly will I die."
A dying youth thus gently pleads,
    Smiling although his end is nigh.
His rule-book in his hands they lay,
    And then his crucifix; and then
The beads, plied briskly many a day,
    They twine round book and cross again.

"Give me my rule-book, beads, and cross"—
    Familiar, faithful friends were these:
The world's gay toys and gilded dross
    He from the first had spurned with ease.
He fervently had told his beads,
    His rule had kept, his cross had borne;
For him now Mary intercedes,
    Who well had served her night and morn.

The rule. To Duty's petty strife
    The rarest worth obedience lent:
A saint, because his daily life
    Was but his rule's embodiment,

The altar-prayer of Berchmans' feast
  Exalts that zeal which greatly prized
The humblest duties and the least:*
  In him the rule is canonised.

The cross. "But my chief cross shall be
  The common life of duty done†
When—how—because it pleases Thee,
  Whose cross for me all grace has won."
Oh, cheerful, meek, unselfish saint!
  Teach us how sad, how sad the loss,
One moment in the fight to faint—
  One moment shun our daily cross.

The beads. "I ne'er will rest until
  For her I feel the tenderest love,‡
Who loved me first, and loves me still,
  With love a Mother's love above."

---

* Minima maximi faciam. St. Francis Xavier used to say: "Be great in little things."

† Maxima mea mortificatio vita communis.

‡ "I shall not be safe until I love the Blessed Virgin with a truly filial affection."

The prayer of Blessed John Berchmans' Mass and Office, to which the third of these stanzas refers, runs thus:—

"Almighty God, who hast established the admirable sanctity of the Blessed John, thy confessor, in his perfect observance of religious discipline, and in the innocence of his life; grant us, by his merits and by his prayers, grace faithfully to observe thy commandments, and thus to attain to purity of soul and body, through Jesus Christ our Lord."

So day by day he says her beads,
   While in his eye the fond tear glistens;
And hour by hour in all his needs
   He cries to her who smiles and listens.

"Give me my beads, my cross, my rule—
   With these, with these I'll die with joy."
Christ hails him perfect in his school,
   A hero-saint—that guileless boy.
Within his wasted fingers pressed,
   Before his failing gaze they lie.
With these three shrined within my breast,
   I too would gladly, gladly die.

MY THREE.

O LOVELY blossoms of a fruitful tree,
   Dear Aloysius, Berchmans, Stanislaus!
   Sometimes, in all my love for you I pause
To think how is it that I love you three.
Saints nearer earth were surely best for me.
   But why should I thus wonder at the cause?
   Is it not one of Nature's ancient laws
That like attracted by unlike should be?

And so I place my special trust in you—
Who are not saints, but angels, to our view—
　And not in those of less sublime degree.
Oh! if that other maxim's true above,
That they who love grow like to what they love,
　Then, blessed Brothers, make a saint of *me*.*

TO ST. JOHN FRANCIS REGIS. (*June* 16.)
[A.D. 1597-1640.]

Few know thy name, St. Francis Regis!† Few
Beyond thy native hills pay homage due,
Save those thy brothers and dear friends, who share
That slandered name it was thy pride to bear.
Nay, some who know thee need to ask thy claim
To shining aureole and saintly fame.
What wast thou? what hast suffered? what hast done,
That 'mid his heroes God hath ranked thee one?
No novice-prince who, yet a boy, hath given
Honour, and wealth, and prouder hopes for heaven—
No hermit hoar, who long, long years hath passed
In lonely watchings and in cruel fast;
No fiery martyr, who hath meek defied
The tyrant at the stake, and smiling died.

---

* Contributed by my kind friend, S.M.S.
† St. John F. Regis is a much more popular Saint than the writer twenty years ago imagined him to be.

TO ST. JOHN FRANCIS REGIS.

Thy story reads not like a wild romance,—
It never strays from polished modern France,
Where, 'mid the rudest of her southern steeps,
Its stream unseen, but fertilising, creeps.
Yet in that homely sphere of some score miles,
What restless, tranquil zeal—what saintly wiles
For luring souls to God! Ah, wherefore roam?
The hero finds a hero's work at home.

Oh, thou hard-toiling missionary-saint!
Not thine in such dull martyrdom to faint.
The winter's ice, men's freezing doubts and sneers,
Chilled not thy glow, but thawed beneath thy tears.
Dauntless in labour, patient to endure,
The firm, the mild apostle of the poor.
Francis and Lewis here in one behold—
Xavier at home, Gonzaga twice as old.*
Oh, gray-haired Aloysius! Yes, that name
When thou wast young, thy virtues well might claim,
Hadst thou, like him, been early snatched away,
Not left to bear the "*burden of the day.*"
But thou liv'dst on, God spared thee to his earth,
Keeping thee innocent as at thy birth,
That first true birth when o'er thy baby-brow
The waters flowed, and left thee pure as snow—

---

* Not quite. St. Aloysius died in his 23rd year, six years before the birth of St. Francis Regis, who lived forty-three years, twenty-six in the Society.

Pure none the less, when, after many a year
Of earnest faith, of humble, loving fear,
After great things for *his* sake done and borne,
God bade the peasant of the Velais mourn,
Mourn for thy loss.

     Oh, great St. Regis, pray
That we, thy brothers, in our meaner way
God's work may do: from many a soul to burst
The glittering fetters of the king accursed.
Teach us to share thy burning, melting love
For Him who on the right-hand reigns above,
Yet hides upon our altars. Oh, great heart!
In thy rich treasures gain for us a part:—
The meekness of thy strength, so gay, so sure—
Thy wistful fondness for God's outcast poor—
Thy yearning for the sinner, hate of sin—
Thy filial pride in her whose breast within
Thy boyhood and thy manhood calmly sped.
Ah! may she lead us on as thou wast led.
She is the same great Mother still; but we,
St. Francis Regis! are not like to thee.

MY SAINTS IN HEAVEN.*

I.—SANCTI.

To those high souls whose changeless lots
    Are laid for aye in heaven's calm mirth,
I dare to lift my yearning thoughts,
    A sinner from this sinful earth.
I gaze, and 'mid that countless host,
    That sing and shine before the throne,
One gallant band attracts me most—
    My eye can rest on it alone.

Its leader bears a martial mien,
    His glance is keen, his forehead broad;
There is the stamp of empire seen—
    He must have done great things for God.
With filial reverence near him stands—
    More like a warrior-king than priest—
Apostle of a hundred lands,
    The wonder-worker of the East.

---

* The first division of this poem refers successively to the canonised Jesuits—St. Ignatius, St. Francis Xavier, St. Francis Borgia (alluding to a well-known incident in his life); then to St. Stanislaus and St. Aloysius, St. John Francis Regis, and St. Francis Jerome. The beatified Jesuits in Part II. are described in this order: Andrew Bobola, John de Britto, the three martyrs of Japan; and then Peter Claver, Alphonsus Rodriguez, and John Berchmans. In Part III. reference is made to Blessed Margaret Mary Alacoque, St. Thomas Aquinas, St. Agnes, St. Mary Magdalene, St. John the Evangelist, and St. Matthew.

And then the duke of name abhorred—
  Oh! he had much and gave his all;
He could not brook to serve a lord
  For whom he soon might bear the pall.
Kneeling close, close to Mary's feet,
  Their arms round one another twined,
Two princely youths of aspect sweet,
  To God win many a youthful mind.
France claims our next: with gentle mien
  Amid her rudest heights he went,
Doing a hero's work unseen,
  By fasting, toils, and vigils spent.
Calabria our latest gave—
  The missioner of golden mouth;
By few yet known or cherished, save
  His brethren and his own fair South.

II.—Beati.

These are the heroes of our race,
  Whose praises through God's temple ring;
Whose costly shrines God's temple grace,
  Whose memories still fresh lustre fling.
But unto others of that band
  Like homage shall ere long be given;
Already some, by Rome's command,
  Are blessed hailed of earth and heaven.

MY SAINTS IN HEAVEN.

Yes, soon among her noblest saints
   The Church will rank that martyr brave,
Whom to a death which he that paints
   Feels his veins chilled, the cossacks gave.
Less brave than he who many a year
   Played the stern Brahmin's painful part,
Waiting in solitude austere
   To win at last the Hindoo heart.
Three martyrs,* strange in garb and air—
   Japan! in these thy children see;
From thee their death, for thee their prayer,
   Yet still to idols bends thy knee.
He, too, whose life's best hopes and prayers
   Were, as the foolish wise might say,
Lost in dull, loathsome, secret cares
   For the poor Negro far away.
Near him his meek old master stands,
   Whose years in lowliest toils did pass;
The well-worn beads are in his hands,
   As when he used to serve at Mass.
And he so late beatified,
   The Belgian youth so gravely sweet;
Oh, may he, to our joy and pride,
   Our trio of boy-saints complete!

---

* Paul Miki, John de Goto, and James Kisai, native Japanese Jesuits and martyrs, were canonized on Whit Sunday, 1862. These lines were written some years before. In the succeeding lines Blessed Berchmans was of course at that date described as "not yet beatified." Many others ought now, thank God, be added to this division of *Beati Societatis Jesu*.

III. Patroni.

I look towards heaven, and on the throng
   That gathers round Guipuscoa's knight,
My eye has gloated fondly long,
   Yet glistens with a fresh delight.
On these with warmer trust I call,
   Striving their watchful love to please;
For, though I praise our God for all,
   My heart feels more at home with these.

Nor from my brethren need my glance
   Stray far for her whose favoured part
'Twas to bid Jesus' knights advance
   The love of his most loving heart.
Him, too, I love to whom Christ said—
   "Well hast thou written—what reward?"
The angel meekly bowed his head:
   "None, none, save thine own self, O Lord!"
Near to the patron saint of youth
   One younger gleams in crystal calm—
The martyr girl of Rome, in sooth
   The Shepherd's own most cherished lamb.
Close to that sinless maiden steals
   The sinner gloriously forgiven;
With heart on fire she raptured kneels
   At her Redeemer's feet in heaven.

Yet nearer to the Lord, who lent
   His own dread name to us, " his least,"
Stands one dear patron more—he bent
   O'er Jesus at the parting feast.
Closest I press to him whose name
   They gave me at the holy font;
Few clients my apostle claim,—
   Ah! let *my* fervour fill the want.

These are my saints. To these, to these,
   My worthless love I gladly pay;
And oft they've heard me, on my knees,
   Say more than here I've dared to say.
These are my saints. And ah! the rest
   Will not be jealous, but pray too.
Help me, O Queen of all the blest,
   To come at last to them and you.

TO MY ANGEL.

Spirit of beauty!
   Lent me as guard,
Hard is thy duty,
   Thankless thy ward:
Fondly thou chidest
   Thy erring child—
Near me abidest,
   While here exiled.

Hard is thy duty
  My soul to guard,
Spirit of beauty!
  Watch o'er thy ward.

Spirit of goodness!
  When I am wild,
Chasten my rudeness,
  Angel most mild!
May my heart's feelings,
  Gentle and free,
Be pure revealings
  Of God and thee.
Bear with my rudeness,
  Angel most mild!
Spirit of goodness!
  Watch o'er thy child.

Spirit of power!
  Baffle the foe
Plotting each hour
  To work me woe:
Evening and morning
  Thou art still near;
Whisper kind warning
  Into mine ear.
And oh! the hour
  When, foiled each foe,
Spirit of power!
  My crown thou'lt show.

ASPIRATIONS.

I.—*At Rising.*

Another day begins for me.
  What day shall be my last?
Grant, Lord, that each new day may see
My heart more pure, more dear to Thee—
  And oh! forgive the past.

II.—*Through the Day.*

Forgive me, Lord, forgive me!
  'Tis all that I can say.
I love Thee: make me love Thee
  More truly day by day.

With all my heart I love Thee and adore.
Lord, make me love Thee more, and more, and more.

III.—*While Falling Asleep.*

Lord Jesus, by that bitterness
  Thou didst endure for me
When Thou wast dying, dying,
  Upon the shameful Tree,
And most when forth thy blessed soul
  Did from thy body go—
On my poor soul have mercy now
  And in its parting throe.*

---

* "Domine Jesu, per illam amaritudinem quam sustinuisti propter me in cruce, maximé quando anima tua benedicta egressa est de corpore tuo, miserere animæ meæ nunc et in egressu suo."—*Cæsarius*, lib. xii. c. 50.

COLOPHON.

HOLY thoughts and tender words
    Are at best mere leaves and flowers,
But the fruits are generous deeds—
    Where, ah! coward soul, are ours?

Quickly, quickly comes the end.
    God forgive what's past and gone!
O Madonna! O my saints!
    Pray for me and help me on.

APPENDIX.

RHYTHMUS AD SS. COR JESU.*

Cor Jesu, cor purissimum,
   Cor ara sanctitatis!
Cor meum purga sordidum,
   Infectum tot peccatis.

Qui movet tibi vomitum
   Auferto hinc teporem;
Infunde novum spiritum
   Et spiritus fervorem.

Cor mite, cor humillimum;
   Cor plenum bonitatis,
Cor tuo da simillimum,
   Da ignem caritatis.

Sed quid? si vel seraphico
   Amore cor flagraret,
Non tamen hoc incendio,
   Non satis te amaret.

Ut ergo te diligere,
   Cor Jesu, possim satis,
Immensum da, quo amas me,
   Ardorem caritatis.

* Translated at page 44.

Hoc, hoc amoris jaculo
  Cor meum accendatur,
Et hujus ab incendio
  In cineres solvatur.

O mors exoptatissima
  Sic mori vi amoris!
Amoris sit cor victima
  Pro corde Redemptoris.

Amore tui moriar,
  Cor Jesu, amor meus,
Ut novo corde ordiar
  Amare te, O Deus!

AD B. V. MARIAM SINE LABE CONCEPTAM.*

Virgo virginum præclara,
Præter omnes Deo cara,
  Dominatrix cœlitum!
Fac nos pie te cantare,
Prædicare et amare,
  Audi vota supplicum.

Quis est dignus laude digna
Te laudare, O benigna
  Virgo, fons carismatum!
Gratiis est tota plena,
Tota pulchra et serena,
  Dei tabernaculum.

O quam magna tibi fecit
Qui potens est et adjecit
  Gratiam ad gratiam!
Qui cœlum terramque regit,
Matrem sibi te elegit,
  Sponsum atque filiam.

* Translated at page 47.

AD B. V. MARIAM SINE LABE CONCEPTAM.

Ante mundum te dilectam
Et præ omnibus electam,
  Cœlorum delicias,
A peccato non redemit
Sed jam antea exemit
  Emptorum primitias.

Virgo vere benedicta
Culpa nunquam es obstricta
  Hocce in exilio;
Sine labe es concepta,
Magno lapsui erepta
  Summo privilegio.

Contendebat certatura
Tunc cum gratia natura,
  Gratia prævaluit,
A peccato præservatam
Immunemque illibatam
  Mire te constituit.

Eva nova novæ legis,
Prælecta summi regis,
  Consors ejus gloriæ;
Tu draconem domuisti,
Forti pede contrivisti
  Victrix caput Satanæ.

Semper fulgens munda stola,
Inter mundas munda sola,
  Ascendisti sidera;
Super agmina sanctorum,
Super choros Angelorum,
  Sceptra geris domina.

Ora nunc a dextris Nati,
Jugo solvat ut peccati

Quos redemit sanguine;
Manus tuæ stillant dona,
Vitæ fac cœlestis bona
Et in nos defluere.

Esto nobis maris stella,
Ne nos fluctuum procella
Navigantes obruat;
Ex qua salus est exorta,
Esto nobis cœli porta
Quæ ad vitam pateat.

Virgo clemens, virgo pia,
Duc secura nos in via
Vitæ per exilium;
Nos, O mater, hic tuere,
Olim istic fac videre
Te tuumque Filium.

Fac, te duce, nos orare,
Vigilare et certare,
Certos tuæ gratiæ;
Funde nobis pia dona,
Custos, mater, et patrona
Sanctæ sis Ecclesiæ.

Fac nos stare fide vera,
Caritate, spe sincera,
Absque culpæ macula;
Gregem tibi sic dicatum,
Jam a patribus sacratum
Protegas in sæcula.

IL NOME DI MARIA SANTISSIMA.[*]

MARIA: lo dico e mi risuona appena
    Sul labbro il nome immacolato e santo,
    Che la doglia del cor si rasserena
    E si rasciuga su questi occhi il pianto.

[*] Translated at page 50.

A mhuire mhathair.

Maria: Io dico ed un' immensa vena
D' ineffabil piacer m' inonda in tanto,
Che l'alma fuori di se stessa mena
Ond' ella di suo stato inforsa alquanto.

Maria : con questo nome io vo sicuro
Infra i perigli, e di destin funesto
Il panroso minacciar non curo.

E quando giunto all' ultimo momento
Fia lo spirto fuggevole, con questo
Nome sul labbro io vo' morir contento.

A mhuire mhathair.*

A Mhuire mháṫair ḋíliſ!
Tá anoiſ do ṁí pó-ġeáṙṙ;
Le fiſ a'ſ le na ainġliḃ
De ṁíoſaiḃ bliaḋna—iſ feáṙṙ.
An mí le éin aġ ceolſaḋ,
Le bláṫa 'ġ deaſuġaḋ an féiſ;
A'ſ úṁlaċt duit-ſe, a Mháṫaiſ.
Tabaiſt doṁan a'ſ duile ġo léiſ.

Maſ ſúd, a Mhuiſe Mháṫaiſ!
An altóiſ ſo, ġaċ lá,
De bſiġ ġuſ abſ leat-ſa
Tá deaſ le móſán bláṫ.
Claonamuid ſíoſ d'a n-oſſáil
A'ſ uſnuiġṫe 'ſ ceolta binn'
Feuċ oſainn, a Mhuiſe Mháṫaiſ,
A'ſ bí aġ éiſdeaċt linn.

* A Sister of Mercy has given us this Irish version of the lines at page 23: "O Mary, dearest Mother."

Deapc anuap, a Mhuipe Mhácaip!
Aip do clainn, ann po a tá,
bideann pmigead aip gnúip na mácap
'nuaip tá eudain eile gan gpéd.
Ip tú bainpíogan na b-flaiteap
ag pmagal paoi glóip go bpát,
Act fóp, a Mhuipe mátaip,
feut opainn ann do gpád.

Aip a fon do glaoid opt, "Mhátaip,"
A'p a tug tú duinn, map a' g-ceudn',
Aip fon do Mhic— ap m-bpátaip—
An t-ainim lán de feun.
Aip fon do gpád ag lapad
Ann do chpoide féin, go píop;
A Mhátaip! bí ap mátaip!
A'p bí map Mhátaip fín.

Oć! deunmuid í go minic—
Cho gpádmap map tá pí—
D'iompóg uainn a púile,
gid bid 'gainn fóp a cpoide:
gan puat, act fóp go bpónac,
Oip tug pinn aippi fat go leop;
Act deun pmigead 'pír, a Mhátaip!
gan feapg cup opt níop mó.

'S an t-pamhpad píop na b-flaiteap,
'na m-bideann map gpian an t-Uan;
'San luatgáip a'p an polup,
'San t-puaimneap pin go ciuin:
beidmid ag gpádugad 'p ag molad
S an áit pin—geal go bpát:
má 'noip, a Mhuipe Mhátaip!
má deapc tú opainn le gpád.

BY THE SAME AUTHOR,
Price 1s. 6d., uniform with this Volume,

EMMANUEL:
A Book of Eucharistic Verses.

⁎⁎⁎ In two years "EMMANUEL" has gone through five editions at home and in the United States. It may be had either handsomely bound and printed on larger paper for eighteen-pence, or in a cheap popular form for sixpence.

"Your very musical and devotional poems will, I am sure, be useful and welcome to many hearts."—*Cardinal Newman.*

"It supplies a want in our devotional poetry."—*Cardinal Manning.*

"I have read them all with the greatest interest, and am heartily glad that you have collected, as into a casket, so many holy thoughts and harmonious utterances."—*Denis Florence Mac Carthy.*

"I have read it very carefully, and many of the poems more than once. Their tone of devotion seems to me very beautiful, uniting fervour with sobriety; and they are expressed at once with simplicity and pathos."—*Aubrey de Vere.*

"Full of grace and beauty. The best religious poetry we have met this long time."—*Dublin Review.*

"Une admirable collection de poésies où sont chantées les merveilles et les douceurs angéliques du Sacrement Eucharistique. 'Emmanuel' devrait être comme une sorte de *vade mecum* pour les âmes qui recherchent l'union constante avec Dieu, surtout avec le Dieu de l'Eucharistie."—*Le Propagateur Catholique.*

"Poems as pretty as they are pious, a graceful tribute to the Blessed Sacrament."—*The Month.*

"It will meet with prompt and warm recognition from all cultured readers. Its merits are of a high order."—*The Nation.*

DUBLIN: M. H. GILL & SON, 50 UPPER SACKVILLE-ST.

EDITED BY THE AUTHOR OF THIS VOLUME.

The Irish Monthly.

A SIXPENNY MAGAZINE OF ESSAYS, TALES, BIOGRAPHIES, SKETCHES, AND POEMS.

The IRISH MONTHLY was begun in 1873. A bound Volume has been published at Christmas each year since then, price Seven Shillings and Sixpence.

The Magazine has been favourably noticed in the *Dublin Review, Spectator, Academy, Tablet, Nation, Weekly Register, Westminster Gazette, Public Opinion, Freeman's Journal, Catholic Times, Boston Pilot*, and many other journals at home and in the United States.

Among the Contributors to the Volumes already published are, Sir Charles Gavan Duffy, John O'Hagan, Q.C., Very Rev. C. W. Russell, D.D., Rev. G. Molloy, D.D., Aubrey de Vere, Lord Emly, D. F. M'Carthy, Miss Rosa Mulholland, Lady Georgiana Fullerton, Very Rev. Dean O'Brien, Mrs. C. Martin, Dr. Mapother, Mrs. La Touche Mr. Wilfrid Meynell, Rev. Joseph Farrell, Miss Attie O'Brien, Rev. W. H. Anderdon, S.J., Oscar Wilde, Ethel Tane, Rev. John Healy, Rev. Edmund O'Reilly, S.J., Rev. D. Murphy, S.J., Rev. Thomas Finlay, S.J., Rev. W. A. Sutton, S.J., Rev. M. Watson, S.J., Mr. Edward Harding, Miss Katherine Roche, Miss Alice Esmonde, Mrs. Bishop, Miss Kathleen O'Meara, Rev. Peter Finlay, S.J., Mr. Nathanael Colgan, and Mr. Henry Bedford, M.A.

The Magazine is sent post free for Seven Shillings a year, paid in advance.

DUBLIN: M. H. GILL & SON, 50 UPPER SACKVILLE-ST.
LONDON: BURNS & OATES; SIMPKIN, MARSHALL & Co.

www.ingramcontent.com/pod-product-compliance
Lightning Source LLC
Chambersburg PA
CBHW020128170426
43199CB00009B/684